What Do I D [illegible] An Introduction [illegible]

N[illegible]

Escapethenarcissist.com

Table of Contents

Chapter One - What is a Narcissistic Mother?

A narcissistic mother isn't something you can describe in a sentence or two; a narcissistic mothers behavior is much more complex than that. There isn't a set description for a narcissistic mother, but rather a number of traits and behaviors she uses to control her child for her own selfish needs and wants.

The reason that a narcissistic mother wants control over her child differs from mother to mother: some want to use their child to make them look superior, some use their child to look after the family, some use their child as a scapegoat for all that's imperfect in their life. Regardless of the 'reason why' she exhibits such selfish behavior towards her child, the feelings of confusion, hurt and rejection remain just as painful for her child.

I'll begin by comparing narcissistic parenting to normal, nourishing parenting.

A nourishing mother is a healthy, loving mother who loves her child without conditions. She puts healthy boundaries in place and offers support, positive reinforcement and aims for her child to grow up to fulfill its hopes and dreams.

A narcissistic mother doesn't do this. *So what does a narcissistic mother do?*

In many cases, the face she shows the outside world is much different from the one she shows behind closed doors. To those on the outside looking in, she will portray herself as a good mother, a devoted and caring wife, an excellent provider for her family; she wants to be viewed as superior to those around her, with a superwoman-like effect on those who marvel at her greatness. The narcissistic mother seeks admiration from others and this is something she needs to feed her fragile ego.

However, as the child of a narcissistic mother, we know the dark secrets she exposes behind closed doors. She can be ill-tempered, easily annoyed and self-centered. She's usually "always right", and can be extremely unpredictable, causing her child to walk on eggshells a lot of the time.

A narcissistic mother can be extremely confusing to understand as a child and growing up. As children, we don't understand the complexities of low self-worth, brittle confidence, and selfishness. We simply have to endure the by-product of those emotions, which is narcissism (I'll touch on this later in the book in the chapter 'Why is My Mother a Narcissist?')

My story may sound a little similar to yours, so if you're still unsure if your mother is narcissistic, maybe finding my story relatable will help.

My mother was a controlling, terrorizing narcissist and my father was a functioning alcoholic who took out his anger on my mother. Of course, any anger my dad released upon my mother undoubtedly fell down the food chain onto me: anytime he berated her or hit her, she would unleash nastiness and venom towards me.

As well as taking her emotions and frustration out on me, she thoroughly terrorized my childhood.

What made this confusing was the times when she would be nice to me and tell me jokes, seeming to enjoy making me laugh and seeing me smile. I would wonder if she just did this to seem like a 'good mother' or try to appease her conscience for all of the other horrible things she said and did.

Sometimes she would buy me nice gifts, but use them against me if I 'upset' or disobeyed her, either by making me feel guilty for her treating me to something or by giving it away. She would sometimes tell people how well I was doing at school, which would make me beam with pride. However, my pride would be short-lived when she would tell me to pretend I got an A grade instead of a C because that's what she'd told people I'd achieved.

I don't remember exactly when she 'became' narcissistic towards me. Of course, her narcissism was there long before I was, but I can't recall when she first treated me with the disdain and nastiness. It was something I had just come to know as normal throughout my childhood.

I was around seven when I perhaps began to really start feeling shy, unworthy, ugly and like I couldn't do anything right. I felt bad for my mere presence most of the time, which meant I sat in my room alone for a big chunk of my childhood. This was picked up on of course, by other family members, my siblings and visitors to the house. They would often try to coax me from my room to sit with the other visitors, but I would do my best to make sure they didn't force me out of the safety of my bedroom. It would mean I would have to be sat with my mother, and I always seemed to do something wrong in front of company to upset her. I would either say the wrong thing, do something she deemed embarrassing or not look well presented enough to be seen by other people, thus making her scream at me when we were alone.

It was simply easier just to sit alone and live inside my head.

I would try my best to please my mother. I would be quiet, get the best grades I could, I'd aim to look as presentable as possible and show her in the best light. I knew if I did those things, she'd be nicer to me. I'd be less likely to be yelled at, ignored or have degrading and belittling things said to me. Keeping on her good side, as well as pacifying her anger towards me, would also make me feel grateful for the 'compassion' she'd show me by not shouting, screaming or mocking me.

When I began to grow a little older, perhaps my very early teens, she began unburdening her life stresses onto me. She would tell me her personal problems, get upset at how people were treating her and tell me things my father had said and done to her that she knew would upset me. She seemed to take pleasure from guiding me towards the more painful things in life, instead of shielding me from them.

Growing up, I was a daddy's girl. Although violent, he was still the 'safe' parent somehow. I stopped being so close to my dad when my mother started revealing the things he'd done to upset her throughout the years. I was around twelve, maybe just thirteen, and I began to despise him. Looking back at my very young self, and the way my mother would act and react when I would play with my father, or simply sit and watch T.V with him, I can see she was riddled with envy. She would demand I went to bed if we were in the middle of a T.V show or tell me to go clean my room if my father and I were playing in the living room.

I recall once she demanded I stop making so much noise or I'll be sent to my room. My father and I were drawing, and he was making me laugh with his caricature of my mother. This obviously riled her, but instead of asking my father to stop drawing unflattering pictures of her (or better yet - laughing with us), she dragged me up by my arm, smacked my bottom and sent to bed. She was eaten up by jealousy. With my father, he came first. Then alcohol. Then me. Then her. She hated that.

Growing up into my teens, I was very insular, shy, unsure and didn't really have an identity of my own. My mother had molded me into that person. I didn't know how to make choices - she made them all for me. What clothes suited me, what college I ought to attend, what type of friends I need, what career path is best suited for me. I was a shell of a human, too afraid to speak up to my mother, but also unsure as to what I would say if I did have the courage to speak up.

Her narcissism continued into my twenties. She'd make me insecure about my relationships, telling me that I was with the wrong person or tapping into the insecurities she's instilled by telling me they were "untrustworthy" or "up to something" behind my back. She'd either hate my significant other or try to form a really close relationship with them, making them keep secrets from me and telling them I was "emotionally unstable".

The manipulation, control, terrorizing, lies and nastiness continued into my adult life. She was still treating me like a child, but I no longer was one. However, I was still acting in such a childlike way because of her, I stood no chance at having a healthy adult life.

It was only when I took a step back at my life that I could see things a little more clearly. She'd destroyed a relationship of mine, made me so doubtful of myself that I couldn't progress at work and instilled a fear of failure into me so deep I was afraid of any kind of decision making. Only when I stood back to view her trail of destruction did I decide that I couldn't let my fearful inner child and my controlling narcissistic mother rule my life any longer.

I searched the web for things like 'controlling mother' and 'emotionally abusive mother', trying to gain some common ground from others who'd had similar experiences to me. After scanning through various articles, I found the word I needed. It perfectly summed up my mother, and finally gave me the tools to break free from the abuse because now I knew what it was: narcissistic.

Chapter Two - The Various Narcissistic Mother Types

As I mentioned earlier, the narcissistic mother is a complex thing to explain; it's not a one-size-fits-all description: there are multiple types of narcissistic mother, each with their own traits, put-downs and methods of manipulation.

Your mother may show traits of all of the types outlined below, or she may be confined to behaving in line with one set

Before any acceptance and healing begin to take place, the first thing you need to do is have a deeper understanding of the narcissism you endured. With narcissism being such a broad term that is being used more commonly these days, it's become almost an umbrella term for different types of narcissistic behavior.

I'm going to show you five different types of maternal narcissism in order for you to gain a better insight as to what type of abuse you suffered as a child and growing up. You may find that your mother is guilty of more than one type of the behaviors I'm going to describe below; this was the case with me also, so don't think that you need to pick just one type of behavior and stick with it. Narcissism is much more complex than that.

The benefit of taking the time to really delve into a greater understanding of the narcissistic parent is that it helps with the rest of the healing process. You arm yourself with the education and a deeper knowledge of the gut-churning treatment you were faced with throughout your life.

When I first delved into seeking answers and closure about the narcissism I was exposed to as a child, I looked into the various types of narcissistic parenting that had already been identified.

I desperately sought out some understanding of the treatment my mother bestowed upon me throughout my childhood and adolescence, scanning various sources to find answers. From books, websites, forums, and magazines, I raked through millions of words worth of reading. I knew I had to create a solid comprehension of maternal narcissism before I flung myself into seeking the inner peace I craved.

This was the beginning of my journey to closure, and now, it's the start of your journey, too.

Rejecting Mother

It's distressing to think that the one person in the whole world who should love, nurture and adore us could reject us. What makes this type of narcissism even harder to deal with is the fact that the rejection is often done purposefully, with words and actions being used to intentionally hurt and/or emotionally wound. This is the case with The Rejecting Mother.

The Rejecting Mother will make her child feel unwelcome and unwanted. She will make sure that her child has to question their self-worth by frequently belittling them and making them feel dumb and out of place. She will often call them names, making them feel inadequate and inferior. This is especially the case especially if the child has siblings, whom the narcissistic mother treats with blatant preference.

If the child of a Rejecting Mother dares to question their mother's treatment of them, it's likely that their plea for love and kindness will be met with more hurtful and rejecting behavior. This can be seen by the mother telling the child to get out of her sight, dismissing their allegations and blaming the child for the way they are treated. It's also likely that the child will be blamed for other problems within the family, often being used as a scapegoat by The Rejecting Mother to make the child feel responsible for issues that are out of their control (i.e. problem siblings, arguing parents or money worries).

Here are some examples of behaviors/treatment you may have been exposed to if you were the child of a Rejecting Mother:

Humiliation.

You were verbally humiliated. You were made to feel embarrassed, ashamed and mortified by the things your mother would say to you. Thinking back to these times now as an adult, you may find that you find yourself wincing at the way she made you feel, and feeling those feelings as an adult likely makes you hurt all over again.

I was frequently humiliated by my mother. She would seize the opportunity to make me look and feel stupid.

One time my mother gave me some money to go to the shop for milk. I was around seven or eight and she gave me a ten-pound note as she didn't have any change. I did as she asked, and bought the pint of milk and arrived home with the change. The shopkeeper had given me the wrong change, either thinking I'd given him a smaller note or simply trying to swindle a young girl out of a few pounds (I hope not).

When I handed her the change, she looked at it and placed it on the table. By this point, we had some family members come to visit. "Count the money on the table," she said in a monotone yet menacing manner. I always struggled with counting and anything to do with maths, but as soon as she asked me to do this I knew I'd gotten something wrong. I was surrounded by cousins and my aunts and uncles as my mother shushed them to make them watch me struggle to count the change. Of course, my counting was incorrect and this incensed her.

She mocked me in front of other family members, scolded me for coming away from the shop with the incorrect change, and when the guests left, she smacked me and I spent the rest of the day and night in my room. I didn't dare leave until the next morning.

The next day, she would only offer me one-word questions or answers. "Breakfast?" she asked me as I sat on the sofa. I shook my head to tell her no. "Fine," she replied and carried on with her morning doing laundry.

Of course, I wanted breakfast, but I was too scared to say yes in case it unleashed another verbal assault.

I was becoming increasingly introverted and isolated due to the way my mother treated me. The verbal humiliations became something that, as an adult, I found myself replaying over and over again in my imagination.

In the safety of my mind, I played out the different ways I would have reacted to my mother should I have been as brave as I am as an adult; in my make-believe scenarios, I would tell her she was a despicable mother and that she didn't deserve me. Do you ever find yourself doing the same thing? Sometimes drifting off to a parallel reality where you say the things you wish you'd said, or you stuck up for yourself and ripped her narcissistic ego to shreds?

It's something of a characteristic we 'rejected children' are left with - we tend to live inside of our heads quite a lot of the time. Just be wary about not letting these make-believe conversations you have with your mother transpire into dark, engulfing thoughts of what you *should* have said - it's very easy to descend down that path, but it only leads to prolonged agony. Don't let yourself wander too far down that path.

Being excluded.

This means that you often felt like you were on the outside looking in. It's likely you were blatantly treated differently from your siblings, who you feel had a much happier, fairer and more loving childhood.

As a child, and as a human being, rejection is one of the most painful experiences we endure. As a child, however, it can be a much more difficult thing to comprehend. Being ostracized by your own mother as a child leaves the door wide open for self-loathing and insecurity to creep in. The emotional trauma of being excluded from something you should wholly be a big part of is difficult to digest as an innocent child.

From family holidays, day trips or weekends spent shopping, I was rarely invited. Being the youngest, my mother would use my young age as an excuse as to why I couldn't come. I was 'too young to appreciate a holiday' and too much 'hard work to drag around the shops', yet I would have given anything to have been invited along.

The *exclusion tactic* that a Rejecting Mother employs works to keep the child feeling worthless, unwanted and full of hopelessness. This heartbreaking treatment from a narcissistic mother has horribly far-reaching effects, and I found myself feeling in a state of despair for a big chunk of my adult life as a direct result of my mothers rejecting behavior.

Being shouted at.

A rejecting mother will often yell and shout, ensuring you become certain that your presence annoys them. It can be little things, such as having the T.V a little louder than they'd like, or leaving some toys laying around on the floor.

A healthy mother would handle this in a way that didn't have a negative impact on her child. She'd simply ask her child to pick up their toys or turn the television down. The rejecting narcissistic mother wouldn't do this. She'd overreact. She'd shout. She'd scream. She'd humiliate and berate her child for such seemingly little inconveniences.

A narcissistic rejecting mother would shout at her child for things that other mothers would simply use as an opportunity to teach their child better behavior. For example, when we were out shopping and I'd ask for ice cream. A healthy mother would decline that request in a calm manner, explaining to her child that there's ice cream at home or that they can have some after supper. For a narcissistic mother, this would incite her rage; she'd yell and scream at her child for having the audacity to ask for something. The same reaction would be seen if her child hadn't cleaned their room to the narcissistic mother's standards. Or if they'd fallen over and grazed their knee. Anything that inconveniences the rejecting mother will invite a hurtful response that is often given to the child in a raised voice.

Walking on eggshells is the norm for most children of narcissistic mothers. The panic and dread that rules the life of a child with a rejecting mother create the foundation for a very nervous and anxious adult.

Withholding love and loving gestures.

One of the most inherent maternal instincts for a mother is to show her child love and affection. The need to nurture and support her child is often simply 'just there'. Hugs, ruffles on the top of the head and kisses on the cheek are something a healthy mother doesn't think twice about giving to her child.

However, this isn't the case for a rejecting narcissistic mother. She doesn't have the desire to give her child affection so freely. If this was the case for you, you may recall the yearning you felt as a child for your mother to just show you that you were loved. I remember the envy I would feel when I saw my peers get hugs and kisses off their mother, and I had rarely gotten anything like that off mine. Even as an adult, that yearning can still weigh heavy on your mind.

The Dependent Mother

The dependant mother is overbearing, intrusive and unhealthily reliant on her child. Her emotional neediness means she's prone to doling out guilt-trips and manipulative tactics. These are used to keep the child close.

My mother wouldn't be described as a dependent mother, but I had a friend when I was growing up who did. At the time, I was often quite envious of the relationship she had with her mother. Her mother seemed to dote on her, and they appeared to be really close. She was a single mother and was bringing up my friend and her bigger brother on her own. My friend rarely saw her dad, so, for the most part, it was just her and her mother.

My friend would take care of her mother. She had arthritis in her hand and wasn't working. This meant she didn't go out too much and relied on my friend to keep her company, even on weekends and evenings when other teenagers were out socializing or studying together. I didn't realize it at the time, but my friend was being guilt-tripped into staying with her mother.

When my friend would manage to convince her mother to let her come and spend some time with me, she'd often call her up and ask her to come home. Something would always happen or 'come up' so my friend would invariably have to leave any social gatherings to go and see to her mother.

Her mother would call her to say she was feeling unwell, or tell her that she'd had a fall. When my friend began to rebel against this, her mother bought her a puppy. She would then begin to use the puppy as a bargaining tool to get my friend to stay with her. If my friend dared to stay out too long, her mother would call her up to say the puppy was poorly, had eaten something it shouldn't or that she was struggling to take care of it alone. Of course, my friend would leave and immediately race back to her dependent mother.

My friend also had to forget about dating. No boys were allowed to contact her. Her mother would check her phone, and delete any numbers she may have had in there that were under boys names.

When I was very young, I thought my friend was extremely lucky to have a mother who loved her so much. I envied the fact that her mother loved spending time with her and would always be coddling her and telling her how special she was. As I grew older, I began to realize that their relationship was extremely unhealthy. Her mother was dependant on her, and was clipping her wings to make her stick around; even if this had detrimental emotional effects on my friend.

Whilst I didn't have a dependent mother, I did see how this dynamic plays out by observing my friend and her mother. In my research of narcissistic mothers, I spent a lot of time analyzing the traits of the dependent type narcissistic mother:

Manipulation.

A dependant mother will use manipulation in order to get her child where she needs them. She may manipulate using silent treatment, guilt-tripping or acting devastated by her child's behavior. This can leave her child often apologizing for their behavior, even when they're not entirely sure that they've done anything wrong.

The dependent mother will use manipulation as a way to puppeteer you and ensure she has explicit control over her child. Should she be called out on her overbearing and draining behavior, she will act hurt and bewildered by the 'accusations'.

Absurdly emotional.

When the dependant mother feels that her control over her child may be slipping, or that they're becoming more independent, she'll become absurdly emotional. She may become hysterical, shouting, screaming and crying. The desired effect this behavior has is to regain an emotional grasp on her child; to make sure the child remains where she wants them.

By making her child feel mean, callous, insensitive and uncaring will make sure they don't stray too far away.

Playing the victim.

A dependant mother will play the victim to ensure her child complies with her needy expectations. For example, the dependant mother may use ailments to manipulate her child into being at her beck and call. She may also use guilt-tripping to show herself as the victim in any given situation.

It's also common for the dependant mother to use her victim mentality to reel her child in with blame-filled phrases such as "I gave up my life to take care of you, why do you begrudge doing the same?" This then heaps blame and guilt onto the child, making them feel indebted to their mother.

Addicted Mother

A child who has a mother who has an addiction, whatever that addiction may be, will not be first on her list of priorities. In most cases, the child won't even be second on that list. First on that list is the addiction, second is the mother herself, and third may be her child. In some cases, the addicted mother may have her partner in third place on the list, followed by her child. Regardless, her addiction will always be number one.

What can make this even more confusing for her child is the lies and broken promises she offers her child. Promises of 'getting better' or being sober, clean or getting her life together are frequently broken. This creates a fragile sense of comfort for the child, and eventually, the child will learn not to trust or believe what their mother promises them. This has dire consequences for the adult child of a narcissist, as they grow up with a distrustful outlook on relationships, and are forever fearful of being let down.

Extroverted Narcissistic Mother

With an extroverted narcissistic mother, the persona she portrays to others hides a dark side that's unleashed when she's not in 'performance mode'. When she's not surrounded by people, guests or peers, the mask slips and reveals the mean, nasty and manipulative persona she reserves for behind closed doors.

This is the place the extroverted mother doesn't need to carry on her outgoing persona; she can be her true self. The extroverted side she reveals in public is a charming, often warm and intriguing character. This side has no malice or threat. However, once that mask drops when no-one is around, it reveals the side that instills fear into her child.

My mother was the extroverted narcissistic type. Her reputation and being liked was highly important to her; more important to her than what her child thought of her, or what kind of example she was setting me. If I said or did anything in public that made her look anything less than the person she wished to portray, there would be dire consequences when we got home.

The Achievement Driven Mother

Growing up, my mother would often compare me to another girl from my school called Michelle. As we were growing up Michelle and I would spend a lot of time together. She lived across the road, so I'd often visit her house to go play. Michelle was rarely allowed around our house, as my mother was paranoid that Michelle would go back to her mother and tell her our house was messy or not as nice as theirs. It was a very clean and tidy home I grew up in, and it was furnished quite well. But my mother was so insecure about other people having more or better than she did, that she wouldn't allow many of my school friends to come round in case they would go back and inform other mothers about the 'state' of our house.

Because of this, if I were able, I'd run across the road to Michelle's house.

Michelle was your typical know-it-all at school; she was always the first to put her hand up to answer teachers questions, always had her homework finished by the deadline, she joined the music groups, learned to play the flute and covered her answers when taking tests.

I thought this was just who Michelle was; achievement focused and afraid of being anything less than 'perfect' with her A grades and love of school. But, it turned out it that Michelle's mother was behind her incessant need for unobtainable achievement.

Michelle was pushed to be the best at everything, and if she wasn't, she would face the harsh punishment of her achievement driven mother.

I witnessed those punishments several times. Anything less than a perfect score on a spelling test ensured Michelle was a bundle of anxiety when handing the spelling sheet over to her pushy mother. In green marker pen, the '9/10' was clearly marked on Michelle's spelling effort. Most children would hand that spelling test to their mother whilst beaming with pride. Not Michelle. Her mother looked at the spelling sheet and then glared at Michelle, a look of *'how could you be so stupid'* creeping up on her face: *"We went through this together! How didn't you get the word 'rhythm' correct? What on earth is that spelling? R-Y-H? Your teachers know you practice spelling with me so they'll think I'M stupid too!"*

I nervously watched on as Michelle was verbally humiliated and berated by her own mother for not getting the perfect score on her spelling test. I knew how deflating, heartbreaking and confusing it was when your mother blames you for their unhappiness or their shortcomings, so I really felt for Michelle. At the time, I didn't know that both our mothers were narcissists, but I resonated with her feeling so utterly hopeless.

Although my mother would berate and mock me for different things to Michelle's mother, the emotional battering we took felt the same.

The achievement driven mother will pressure her child to excel, pushing them to achieve more than their peers. Anything that isn't deemed a high standard or grade will ensure that the child is made to feel inferior, an embarrassment or stupid.

With the achievement-driven mother it's often be found that they are living vicariously through their child. Usually, they haven't gotten as far in life as they had hoped or dreamed for, so they have a burning need to live their dreams through her child - regardless of the negative emotional consequences it has on her child.

The achievement driven mother wants to appear to have a superior life to her peers, taking drastic measures to ensure her life looks idyllic to the outside world. An underachieving child would ruin that front, so this type of narcissistic mother will ensure her offspring accomplish things she can brag about.

The fear of the shame of having a less than perfect child is enough to make achievement driven mother cast the emotions of their child to one side in favor of her own selfish wants.

Chapter Three - The Effects of Having a Narcissistic Mother & Ways to Heal As An Adult

Adult children of narcissistic mothers are often left with a barrage of emotional baggage from their emotionally unsteady upbringing. The confused, afraid, unsure and self-doubting child grows up with a wide array of emotional traits that are a direct result of their childhood. When we are growing up, we look to our mothers to guide us through the world and show us right from wrong. We take what they say as the gospel truth and we seek validation and love from them. When these things are in short supply or are absent, it can be utterly confusing for a child to understand, let alone learn what healthy emotions are.

Effect #1: You Have Insecure Attachment.

The narcissistic mother brings you up with you not fully grasping if she loves you or not, and often she would dangle her love over your head in return for your compliance or accomplishments; how could you be expected to develop into an emotionally secure adult with an upbringing like that?

After all, the person who is supposed to provide you with the love and security you need growing up wasn't all that good at it, or interested enough to give it.

As a result, insecurity is one of the biggest plights adult children of narcissistic mothers have to overcome. You are doubtful of yourself and your decision-making skills, you are insecure in your adult relationships and you are paranoid that your friendships aren't solid.

The majority of people who weren't exposed to narcissism or abuse growing up will go on to have a secure attachment in their adult relationships: meaning they feel a healthy amount of comfort and security when they let someone get close to them. Because a narcissistic mother doesn't show you that your feelings can ever be safe in the hands of another person, you go on to become insecure about getting close to people.

This insecurity can be seen in two variations, which I'll outline below:

Avoidant attachment, which means we avoid letting anyone close enough to hurt us and end up having an emotional wall up. Avoidant people tend to be able to distance themselves from their partner easily, and can shut down their emotions quickly if they feel they are being compromised.

Anxious attachment means someone who chases love and security, often quite aggressively, in the hope that their fears of being unlovable will be quashed. However, should they be rejected, the person will become anxious that their fears have been validated, and thus anxiously continue to chase love.

I was most certainly the latter, and anxious attachment is the best way to describe my relationships during my twenties. My fear of loss and rejection ensured that I put up with a lot of abuse and hurt from the relationships I fought for, and my insecurity stopped me from fully understanding my self-worth, which left me trapped in a cycle of anxious attachment.

Do you feel like you may have some insecure attachment issues stemming from your childhood? If so, what type of attachment description do you think best fits you? It's been found that the way in which your mother abused you can match up with a certain attachment description. If you were neglected, berated and withheld love and affection, there's been a correlation with that type of abuse and to the avoidant attachment type. If your mother offered you conditional love or unpredictable attention, it can mean that you likely lean more towards anxious attachment.

Ways to Manage Insecure Attachment

It's no easy task to simply rewire your brain into stopping your insecure attachment. It's something that takes practice, patience and a heap of mindfulness. But, you can most certainly do it.

I was a textbook case of the insecure attachment type. In fact, I probably leaned more towards the extreme side of things. I was forever anxious, had an extreme fear of intimate relationships and never felt at ease or safe when I was in one.

However, I'm now comforted by the fact that even though I was once burdened with relentless insecure attachment, I'm now (more or less) over it. Just a mere couple of years ago, I would never have expected to be able to say such a thing. Accepting my attachment issues and acquainting myself with the debilitating effects helped spur me to make sure I battled against those negative emotions.

When overcoming the negative effects of a narcissistic upbringing, it's wise to remember that whatever was instilled into you by your mother as a child can be rectified as an adult. It does take a little work, some mindfulness, and compassion, but you can certainly release the negativity you're carrying from your childhood.

In moments of attachment insecurity, many of us switch to younger states. We disconnect from present-day resources, reacting not to our partners but instead to our narcissistic mother, who left us feeling so unwanted and rejected.

The first hurdle in overcoming our insecure attachment is identifying it.

There are a few primary ways to alter your attachment style. One is by ensuring you get into long-term relationships with people who have a healthier attachment style than your own. As you may know all too well, this can be much easier said than done, especially if you have esteem issues, and seek out those who are avoidant and emotionally shut down.

You can also overcome the issue of insecure attachment by making sense of your past through writing a coherent narrative. A coherent narrative is a story that makes sense of one of the traumas you've been through. Describe what happened in the traumatic incident and how you felt. Then write about how you think this event impacts you in your life today.

You should write it out rationally, autobiographically, intuitively (meaning including things you *think* happened), and make sure you write about how your past influences your present. Make sure your finished narrative is balanced and completed with self-compassion.

Writing this coherent narrative will help you understand how your childhood experiences are still affecting you in your life today. When you create a coherent narrative, you actually rewire your brain to cultivate more security within yourself and therefore your relationships.

Effect #2: You Blame Yourself.

Narcissistic mothers don't tend to take blame or criticism very well - but they are apt at dishing it out.

Growing up, you likely found that your mother wasn't able to accept blame very well, often refusing any responsibility. Instead, she would project that responsibility onto others; usually you or your siblings or other family members.

A narcissistic mother often deflects her responsibility or part to play in a situation and will instead insist that her child 'made her do it' or forced her into behaving in such a way.

Looking back now as an adult, it's clear to see that during times like this, the narcissistic mother knew she was in the wrong, but she hated to allow something bad be her fault; she would rather let someone else feel the weight of blame.

Some narcissistic mothers even blame their child for the abuse they endure, using phrases such as "don't make me hit you" or "you only have yourself to blame for this". Some children are used as their mothers scapegoat, bearing the heavy burden of blame for the things that are going wrong in her life: her lack of career, her failing relationship, her messy house or her terrible migraines - whatever she felt bad about in her life at that time, it's likely her child was often blamed as the root cause.

I recall times my mother would yell at me, smack me and scream at me to "get out of her sight" as she blamed me for things I had no control over. Things like my sister not getting the washing off the line before it rained (I should have reminded her), the time I fell over and grazed my knee and cried (I should watch where I'm going) or the time she forgot it was non-school uniform day and sent me to school in my uniform (I made her look stupid in front of other parents, so I got a slap across the legs.)

This chronic blame is confusing for a child because we believe what our mother says is true: that we are to blame. However, what's even more confusing is that we didn't really do anything in order to deserve the blame, so guilt and blame become very complicated and confusing emotion to digest as we grow up.

As we are evolving into adults, this unhealthy relationship with blame becomes something we use to try to find comfort and acceptance. We'll blame ourselves for things that aren't our fault, hoping that our emotional sacrifice will make people like us, as we've spared their emotions to the detriment of our own.

For example, the first real relationship I had was an abusive one. For a long time, I would blame myself for the dismal state of the relationship. "Maybe if I was smarter, he wouldn't call me a dumb bitch anymore. It's my fault he gets angry at me because

I'm so stupid", I'd think to myself. Or "maybe if I acted happier to see him, he wouldn't criticize my miserable face anymore". Whatever the issue, I'd make sure I placed the blame on myself before I even dared to think about the alternative - that my partner was the issue. I couldn't deal with the possible painful truth that my partner didn't love me, and to admit to myself that I had been suffering a lifetime of emotional abuse was too much to comprehend for my fragile state of mind at the time.

If you find yourself taking the blame for things that aren't your fault, or constantly heaping blame onto yourself, it's likely you do it for the same reasons I did for so long. Of course, the root of it all began with the way our mothers treated us, but as an adult, that self-blame readjusts: we no longer accept blame just to pacify others. We now blame ourselves for others behaviors and feelings to preserve a cluster of hope that it can change. Self-blame is really a mechanism we use to maintain a sense of control in what can feel like a tough emotional terrain.

Not only can self-blame help us cope with the emotions we encounter as an adult, giving us that sense of control, it's also something we can use to explain away our abusive childhood. We create an illusion that we were to blame and therefore have control over the abuse.

How to Stop Blaming Yourself

When I first discovered my incessant tendency to self-blame, I immediately sought out ways I could counteract this. These are the techniques and mind shifts I made in order to overcome the draining effects of self-blame and banish the negative blameful thoughts from my mind altogether.

Distinguishing the difference between taking responsibility and self-blame.

Noting how your actions and inactions and words left unspoken contribute to an outcome in a particular situation creates a very different account than the one that uses self-blame.

Take some time to think about the aspects of something that's happened recently that didn't end as you'd hoped it would. Go over the factors that led to the outcome.

For example, let's say that a relationship of yours has ended badly. If you have a tendency to self-blame, your initial reaction would probably be: "of course they didn't want me. I'm just not that loveable", or something along those lines. In order to tackle self-blame, you need to take a step back and focus on what each of you brought to the relationship. Instead of automatically placing blame on yourself, think of how each of you contributed to the outcome of the relationship. Their controlling behavior? Their lack of thoughtfulness when it came to you?

This is a healthier way to look at an outcome that you'd usually blame yourself for. Instead of pinning blame, you're attributing an outcome (however undesired) to certain factors. They may or may not be within your control, but regardless, it's a much more stable approach to situations where you're prone to self-blame.

Correct the self-critical voice.

The negative put-downs you give yourself are often an echo of things your mother used to say to you as a child and growing up. It's imperative that this gets tackled as soon as possible.

Begin by making a list of things you like about you. Even if you think you can't create a list of good qualities, or even if you're sat with a pen and paper for half an hour before you can think of something; please try this exercise.

Note down qualities you like about you, abilities you have or skills you've acquired. Any personality traits, quirks or things about you that you think are good - jot them down. Try looking at you from the perspective of a friend. It can be tough but have enough faith in yourself that people do see great qualities in you.

When the critical self-talk begins, talk back to it, using the list of qualities you've created. Talk over and above it. Silence it with your words of self-compassion. When your self-talk tells you that you're stupid, not worthy, unlovable... you can hush those negative words by talking back. Do this every time the negative self-talk begins. Over time, your mind will shift, and the current habit of putting yourself down will be supplemented by the great things you know you have to offer.

Seeing yourself wholly.

Self-blame is founded by reducing yourself to a number of character flaws and letting them define you and who you are. This is instead of seeing yourself as a whole person; like a three-dimensional being. Essentially, when you don't see yourself wholly, you're demoting yourself to being a cardboard cutout version of yourself.

Try to step back, and see yourself with more clarity. If you can, ask some friends about how they see you. Ask for uninhibited honesty, and take the complex answers in your stride. You may be surprised, but it's a good thing to seek out the honest answers of how those close to you perceive you.

Self-compassion.

Do not confuse self-compassion with self-pity. Self-compassion is a non-judgemental view of yourself, your actions, inactions, and weaknesses. It's offering yourself kindness, not judgment.

It's understanding that your actions and reactions are no different from the way other people act or react. You're human like everyone else, and you ought to understand that you will respond in a human way. Don't single yourself out as being lesser than other people. Having compassion for yourself means having painful feelings and now allowing them to engulf or overwhelm you.

Evaluate your beliefs about the self.

How do you see a person's character? Do you view the personality as set in stone, or do you think it's capable of changing? How you view the self often affects how you act and think, as well as being a good indicator as to how you will recover from hurtful events. If you think you can change, or if you think things are set in stone, these beliefs will affect how you will recover from rejection, upset and painful memories.

Effect #3: You Have a Tendency to Self-Loathe.

Growing up with the feeling of never being enough or 'good enough' takes its toll on the adult child of a narcissistic mother. When your mother makes you feel that you can't do anything right or like you're a burden to her or like you're stupid, it's hard to shake those feelings away, even as an adult.

Stemming from the feeling that if you can't make the one person in the world who's supposed to love us unconditionally care about you, what hope do we have to make anyone else happy? This helpless feeling that there must be something wrong with us mutates into an ugly feeling of self-loathing as an adult.

Because we can feel unworthy, blameful towards ourselves and often downright unlovable, we become a breeding ground for self-loathing thoughts and actions.

The gut-churning memories of my childhood often stopped me from even liking who I was, let alone loving myself. My mother always compared my looks to those of my older sisters, who were very pretty and made the most of their striking looks. They'd always look effortlessly beautiful, and my mother made sure they and everyone else was aware of that. However, I was always made to feel like the ugly duckling who my mother was ashamed of. I remember one time she apologized to one of her friends for my appearance and told them "I'd not been blessed with my sister's flair for fashion, silky hair or flawless skin." She ran her fingers through my hair as she laughed about it, as if I was in on the joke and was laughing too. I was mortified and ashamed of myself. I wanted the ground to swallow my ugly self up.

I recall that day as being the instigation of me really hating the way I looked. I was around twelve years old. As a child, I would look in the mirror and hope to transform into a beautiful adult. After all, my mother said I might grow out of my ugly phase, although my sisters never had that ugly phase, so she couldn't be sure. As an adult, I would look in the mirror and loathe what was looking back. I believed for so many years that I was ugly and therefore someone to be hidden away, ashamed, and someone who is less of a being that those who are seen as beautiful.

As our sense of self is developing as a child, it can be profoundly traumatic to have to endure the backlash of emotions that come with a narcissistic upbringing. Shame, embarrassment, blame, guilt, fear... they all combine to create a cesspit of self-loathing for the adult child.

Ways to Tackle Self Loathing

Growing up with a narcissistic mother means we're burdened with messages that we're not good enough - not smart enough, funny enough, attractive enough - we take in those insults and the rejectful behavior we endured and we believe it. We take the hurtful lies about our self-worth and think they're the truth, which eventually leads to self-loathing.

Overcoming this step was undeniably difficult for me, but I managed. I made sure to keep the following in mind:

<u>Don't live in the past or the future.</u>

You've probably heard this before, and it's hard to do, I'll admit, especially when you have bundles of anxiety to contend with.

However, self-loathing can't touch you if you're living in the present. If you're not in the present, you're obsessing over the past of things could have done, or you're worrying about future events. It's a mental trap that's caught most of us, but you can escape by living in the present. When you find the self-loathing creeping in, take a deep breath and bring yourself back to the present. Drop the self-loathing baggage and just be in the here and now.

Befriend your demons.

It may sound counterintuitive, but as the saying goes: keep your friends close, and your enemies closer. This is just as true for your inner demons.

Getting to know the side of yourself that you don't like needn't be scary; it can be fascinating. Face them head-on. Be curious, kind and gentle to them. Everybody has demons, but it's how we handle our demons that really matters. Instead of ignoring your demons, acknowledge them (without judgment).

Question your beliefs and thoughts.

The majority of us accept our thoughts as truth, without question. However, just because we've thought of something as truth or fact for the past twenty years, doesn't make it the truth. To really fight back against self-loathing, start to question the automatic thoughts and beliefs you have. Come up with logical, realistic alternatives.

Embrace compassion.

Often, attacks of self-loathing come raging in after we feel we've done something incorrect, wrong or 'bad'. Maybe we drank too much, ate too much, or done something we shouldn't have. Forgive yourself for your mistakes. Attacking yourself only sustains the cycle. Self-loathing and shame don't stop or correct unwanted behavior. More often, simply, they fuel the fire instead.

Acknowledge that you're a human who makes mistakes. Aim to move forward in a positive way, with a newfound sense of compassion.

Make the effort to get to know someone you envy.

Being a child of a narcissistic mother, self-loathing often means you're prone to social comparison: So-and-so is better looking than I am, richer than I am, more popular than I am — *just BETTER than I am.* But when you get to know someone on a more personal level, you get to see them for who they are, flaws, imperfections, insecurities and all. Perspective is everything, and it's so important to understand that we're all imperfect.

Collect good feelings.

When someone says something nice about you, make a note of it. Not just a mental note, try to keep a journal or a notebook if you can. When you have the courage to try something new, write it down in that notebook too. When something fantastic happens, write it down. This way, you're collecting good thoughts and moments, almost like souvenirs. You can store these little notes in a box or jar. When you're feeling low or like you want to do something destructive, pull it out. Read through the good feelings and remember them all over again.

Effect #4: You Self-Sabotage.

Being on the receiving end of maternal narcissism, you come to accept the notion that disappointment and being misunderstood are feelings that are certain in life. Good things that may happen to you are likely to be soon stipped away once the universe notices that you've somehow gotten lucky, so in order to stop yourself being hurt when that happens, you self-sabotage.

Self-sabotage is another protective cloak we children of narcissistic mothers wear in order to protect ourselves. If we don't express our care for someone else, or even better, if we simply cut them off, we reduce our chances of being hurt. If we hurt them before they hurt us, which they will, we can offer ourselves some damage control when they do eventually disappoint us. It's this way of thinking that ensures our already fragile emotions aren't toyed with.

Self-sabotage doesn't just occur in relationships either, it comes in many other self-destructive ways. You may exhibit lazy behaviors and not push yourself to greater things as you're fearful of humiliation or rejection. You may allow yourself to become embroiled in toxic situations. You may care so much about what others think of you that you don't live the life you want. You may surround yourself with people who don't have your best interests in mind.

What self-sabotage essentially boils down to is the adult child, who endured harmful narcissism during the most emotionally crucial years of their life, becoming a self-fulfilling prophecy. The tendency to sabotage good things comes from the confidence-crushing words of the narcissistic mother and causing them to become true: "you're dumb", "you're worthless", "you don't deserve good things", are all beliefs instilled into the child as they are growing up. Consequently, the adult child turns this belief into behavior.

Can you think of any self-sabotaging behaviors that you exhibit? They may be so subtle that you have to really have a deep think to find them. For me, my self-sabotage wasn't so subtle; I would end relationships, seemingly out of the blue for my partner. They'd have no idea what they'd done wrong - often nothing. I'd be so self-deprecating about my looks in order to stop other people from making horrible comments - you can't hurt someone who already acknowledges their faults. Little did I understand that no-one would make any horrible comments; I wasn't the "creature" my mother made me feel like I was. But any compliments given to me were shot down with self-deprecation, which only added further bricks to my emotional wall.

I would avoid putting myself up for promotions at work to avoid rejection and disappointment, or for fear of being exposed as a fraud.

If you've discovered that you harbor some self-sabotaging tendencies, it's important to remember that this defense mechanism is destructive, not protective.

Tackling Self-Sabotaging Behavior

"You can't do that!" or "that's way too difficult!" may sound familiar to you. "If you try, you'll probably just fail anyway" may be another phrase your familiar with. These statements may sound as if they're coming from a ruthless and cruel person with a sole purpose to destroy your self-confidence. They stemmed from your childhood to manifest into a destructive pattern of behavior. Sadly, far too often, we can be the ruthless sabotager, and our target is often ourselves.

The self-loathing talk can lead to self-sabotage and can stop us achieving our goals and dreams.

What makes it worse is that we usually don't see that it's happening. Instead, we will attribute our lack of success or productivity to inadequacy. This then boosts the negative messages we supply ourselves, ensuring we get caught in a self-sabotaging cycle of behavior.

A telling sign that you are self-sabotaging yourself is when you grind to a halt when you're trying to achieve your goals, for no logical reason. The ability and desire are there: but something stops you moving forward.

When you feel like you can't do something that you should be able to, or that you shouldn't do something, even though you know deep down that you want or need to do it, this is self-sabotage at work.

There are some common themes in self-sabotaging behavior:

Knowing you should be working on something, but putting it off again and again.

Starting projects, but seeing them through.

Feeling unmotivated or unable to continue, even when there are lots of exciting opportunities.

Unfulfilled ambitions.

Fretting over things that really don't really matter.

Worrying that if you fail, others will think less of you.

Doubting yourself and your ability.

Feeling stressed and anxious, suffering from unexplained depression or panic attacks when trying to achieve something.

Using aggressive communication and not taking steps to change this.

Ruining relationships with others due to anger, resentment or jealousy.

Diminishing your own achievements.

Taking even unfair or misguided criticism to heart.

Allowing others to put you down.

Whatever your own self-sabotaging behavior is, you must overcome it if you are to defeat the effects of your childhood. Too many children of narcissists or abusive parents fall into the trap of living with the aftereffects of an abusive childhood, not realizing that they needn't feel the way they do. No longer children, you're now an adult with the powers to change your situation and your mindset.

Breaking the cycle of self-sabotage begins with your thinking. Recognize your self-sabotaging behaviors, and ask yourself:

What goals have you had for yourself for a long time and never been able to accomplish?

What do you consistently fail at, for no obvious reason?

Are there particular areas where you find yourself procrastinating or putting off making a decision?

Are you suffering from lack of motivation to do something that you want to do?

Do you find yourself unreasonably angry or frustrated, and is this affecting your relationships?

Is there an area where other people (such as your boss) consistently get frustrated with you?

Is there something in your life that nags at you and causes you dissatisfaction because you know you could do it, or do it better?

Ask yourself questions like these, and tune in to the situations where you may be sabotaging yourself. Monitor your behavior, and think about the above questions.

The perfect time to do this is when you're engaged in sabotaging behavior. As you're doing so, monitor your 'stream of consciousness' and write all the negative thinking going on whilst you're self-sabotaging.

If this isn't feasible, use imagery to recreate the situation in your mind so that you can experience the automatic thoughts, recalling what you were thinking last time you engaged in that destructive behavior.

Effect #5: You Have a Hard Time Setting Boundaries.

When your own mother won't take "no" for an answer or respect your wishes, why would anyone else?

If you grew up as a pawn in your mother's quest for superiority, or you were used as a maid or caregiver, or if your mother was terrifyingly demanding, chances are you shy away from the word "no".

Because of this, it can mean you grow up being everybody's punching bag, worrying yourself about other people and their needs before your own. You develop into an adult who has difficulty setting boundaries with those around them. Boundaries are simply an acknowledgment from you about what you want, and what you don't want. This impacts how you are willing to allow yourself to be treated or not treated.

The thought of setting boundaries can induce panic and anxiety to adult children of abuse.

For years I set little to no boundaries with friends and especially in relationships. My default setting was to put other people's wants and feelings above my own. I felt anxiety at the mere thought of telling someone "no" or letting them know that it was unacceptable to treat me so disrespectfully.

Setting Boundaries

I understand that it isn't easy to set boundaries with toxic people, but it's something we can all learn to do. Trust me when I say that when we do, it's empowering.

To set boundaries means to take care of ourselves and ensure our emotional health is being protected. By setting boundaries, we're less stormy and resentful towards others because our needs are getting met. Making boundaries means we make our expectations clear, letting others know what to expect from us and how we expect to be treated.

Boundaries create a solid foundation for healthy and happy relationships.

Of course, growing up with a narcissist means that setting boundaries isn't one of our greatest strengths. In fact, we're used to any boundary we try to put in place being dismissed ignored or simply just brushed aside as us being 'difficult'. In some cases, the narcissistic mother will attempt to violate boundaries in especially harmful ways: she may argue, blame, threaten or manipulate until we relent. I understand we can't control how other people act or behave towards us, but we can learn to set our boundaries and stick to them.

To begin, make sure you identify the boundaries you wish to put in place. Be clear on what you need before trying to communicate or enforce that boundary.

Communicate your boundaries or expectations clearly, calmly, and (perhaps most importantly), consistently. Stick to only the facts without getting yourself flustered or feeling like you have to explain yourself. Try not to blame, get frustrated or become defensive. This will only lead to you feeling emotionally drained and full of negative emotion. For example, it's more effective to say "I'm going to leave now. I'm not going to argue with you," than to lose your temper and say "stop trying to argue with me - you're always making me feel so useless and incompetent, stop shouting at me like that!"

When our boundaries aren't respected, we need to step back and evaluate our options. From here we can take action.

Setting boundaries is an ongoing process and there isn't a quick fix for dealing with those who violate those boundaries. We can't force people to respect the boundaries we put in place, but we can control how we respond to them if they choose not to respect our boundaries. The following ideas can help you choose the best approach for dealing with those who insist on violating the boundaries you have in place.

Firstly, is the boundary you're wanting to put in place negotiable? Some boundaries are more crucial to your mental health than others, so it's wise to consider if you can see yourself ensuring that you'll enforce it consistently.

Establish what you're willing to accept and think about what you would consider non-negotiable or a deal breaker. This should help you decide if you're willing to compromise on certain boundaries. Sometimes a compromise can actually be a healthy thing, especially if you and the other party are only just adjusting to the newfound boundaries that are in place. Genuine compromise isn't about abandoning your own needs to ensure you're pleasing others or accepting ill-treatment for an easier life.

If you find that someone is repeatedly violating your most necessary and important boundaries, you need to think about how much longer you're going to accept that poor treatment. It may be that you're accepting of any abusive behavior or boundary violation you receive because you're hoping that the toxic person will somehow change in the future. I've seen it happen time and time again, and I'm confident you'll look back on yourself in some years to come and see that the person you hoped would miraculously change had no intention of ever changing their ways or respecting your boundaries.

I implore you to set boundaries and, just as crucially, stick to them - even when you want to cave in and allow yourself to compromise on your emotional needs. Try to write down what's happening. This is a way to record any boundary violations. Also be sure to note your responses to these violations - this will help you find any weaknesses in your boundaries as well as help you evaluate your reactions to any boundary violations.

It's hard to set the same boundaries repeatedly with somebody who isn't listening, and all too often we'll give up and become lax and inconsistent with our boundaries. If you notice that you're not consistently putting healthy boundaries in place, make the required adjustments and aim to stick to these consistently.

If you're being consistent by jotting things down, this can help you get some clarity on what you're willing to accept and show you the fruits of your boundary setting. Another important thing to keep in mind is that you'll need to accept that some people will simply not respect the boundaries you wish to implement. This is a very difficult and sometimes painful truth to accept because we'd like to be able to be strong enough to make sure people respect our boundaries. It can be discouraging to think that you're just someone's ego-inflating push around, and it's disappointing to conclude that you may need to think about whether you should continue having a relationship with somebody who chooses to ignore your boundaries.

You can't change someone else's behavior, as frustrating as this is to come to terms with. You can, however, choose to accept ill-treatment and boundary violations, or you can opt to disengage. It's also a good idea to practice the idea of loving detachment. Detaching is a side step away from trying to control other people and situations. When you're in a state of absolute fear or panic, it's understandable that you'd want to control things to protect yourself and ensure the outcome isn't an unpleasant one. However, trying to control other people and their actions never ever works.

When we learn to detach, we're stopping the need to change others, as well as learning that we can't force the outcome that we want. It's often a fruitless waste of our time to even try and force things to happen how we want anyway.

You can practice detaching from a narcissist or toxic person by:

Physically leaving a situation especially if it's uncomfortable or potentially dangerous responding in a different way. For example, instead of taking something personally or reacting by shouting, you can instead choose to shrug off a rude or unwanted comment and not acknowledge it. This changes the dynamics of the conversation or interaction and cuts the supply for the narcissist. It lets the narcissist then make their own choices and then deal with the consequences of those choices.

Detaching also takes your mental energy away from an unproductive conversation or argument, which is good for your emotional health, especially if it's an old rehashed argument you've had before. Detaching doesn't mean you don't care about this person; it simply means you're taking care of you. To take care of you as best you can, you need to think about what you can do in each volatile or negative situation.

Consider the option of limiting contact or going no-contact all together. In some cases, the only way to protect yourself is to stop spending time with people who don't respect you. Limited or zero contact isn't meant to punish or manipulate others, even if they try to suggest that's what you're doing by cutting contact with them. It's a form of emotional self-care. If someone is hurting you, be it physically or emotionally, you owe it to yourself to make some distance between you and this toxic person.

You don't have to have a relationship or maintain contact with family members who make you feel bad about yourself, put you down and are abusive towards you. Family and friends should support you and uplift your spirit, not leave you feeling depressed, anxious, upset frustrated or confused.

One of the great things about being an adult is that we now have choices. You don't have to continue being in a relationship with someone who chooses to take advantage of you or your gentleness, nor do you have to work for someone who belittles you and manipulates you. As an adult, we now have choices and it's important to understand that we have them, and we can make full use of that luxury that we didn't have as children. We aren't trapped or powerless anymore.

Effect #6: You Have Trust and Abandonment Issues

The fear of abandonment was a huge issue for me. Escaping this crippling fear was one of the biggest breakthroughs I had when I was recovering from my childhood emotional abuse. It's a huge symptom of maternal narcissism, and it's something many adult children carry with them for their entire lives if they don't acknowledge it as an issue.

It almost goes without saying that trust is also a factor that ties in heavily with this effect; we have such deep trust issues that the thought of anyone caring about us enough to stick around, emotionally or physically, seems like a long shot. This anxious fear of abandonment that we're left with doesn't just affect relationships, either. It can have a profound effect on our life choices and decisions, often pushing us towards choices that aren't in our best interest, but rather choices that suit other people.

Being raised by a narcissistic mother sets the scene for your self-worth as an adult. A narcissistic mother brings her children up with them having a warped sense of what their emotional needs are, and what it means to be validated. Her children are lied to, manipulated, yelled at, mocked, made to feel worthless. These toxic feelings then evolve with us as we grow, and become twisted anxiety that can really affect relationships.

The fear of abandonment can rear its ugly head in the form of: being envious of your partner, giving too much of yourself to your partner, suspecting your partner of cheating on you, or settling for an abusive relationship for fear of being alone. It can also been seen if you worry about your partner leaving you alone for too long or stressing if they have to leave, or it may mean that you develop separation anxiety when you're apart from them.

The emotional abandonment we received as a child, however consistent or intermittent, has a huge part to play in the trust and abandonment issues we have as adults. We're afraid that the same cold feelings of abandonment that shattered us as children will happen to us from other people who are supposed to love us.

Overcoming Abandonment Issues

The first thing you need to start affirming to yourself is this: you are worthy of love. Everyone is. There's no such thing as a perfect person. We all want to love and to feel loved and secure. We all have flaws. Therefore, logic states that love involves two flawed individuals. Each is just as worthy of love.

This doesn't mean that everyone needs to love you; that's unrealistic. When you do find that someone, remind yourself that you're worthy of love and positive attention. Reciprocate and care for the relationship. However, don't allow it to become your identity or the center of your worth - that can be all to easy to do when you're struggling with abandonment issues.

Become emotionally self-sufficient.

Don't allow your identity to be tied to a relationship. Of course, it's part of who you are, but it doesn't define you. Make sure you can embrace this idea and know that you can be okay if you were to be single or be alone. Don't base your worthiness on someone else, or rely on a relationship to validate your worthiness. Instead, you are worthy because you are yourself. No one else can be a better you.

Becoming emotionally self-reliant won't come easy if you've been emotionally dependent on your current or past relationships. Becoming emotionally self-sufficient doesn't happen instantly, so be gentle with yourself when you're going through the process. Take it one day at a time, and keep reminding yourself of these things: you are responsible for your own emotions, and you're still an individual whilst in a relationship.

Remember that it's not another person's job to make you feel stable or emotionally secure. Your emotional security must at first come from you. You are an individual first and foremost, then a partner second. In reminding yourself of these things, take ownership of your own emotions and feelings. When fear, panic or anxiety starts to surface, address those feelings rather than turning them into the unhealthy behaviors of jealousy, giving too much in the relationship or worrying yourself with thoughts of your significant other leaving you.

To summarise what it means to be emotionally self-sufficient, it's very much taking responsibility for your emotions and doing so in a healthy way. It's no longer looking to your significant other to make you feel secure in the relationship. It's not their job to make you feel secure in the relationship because they can't take away your fear.

Accept that some level of fear may always exist within you. To be human means to feel fear. You may never fully eliminate your fear of abandonment, but you can control your reactions to the fear, as well as manage the levels of fear you struggle with.

It's important to identify when you're having those fearful moments in your relationship. For example, the moments of fear that cause you to want to control who your partner is looking at, where they may be going or what they're doing without you there to oversee. You have to identify the unhealthy patterns of thought and understand where the root of that fear is based - from your unstable and emotionally confusing childhood. You don't ever want to feel that pain again.

The fear of abandonment is so deep-rooted, which is a natural human emotion to cope with pain. You can help yourself lessen its toll on you by not allowing it to control your thought patterns and behaviors any longer.

Stop looking to your partner or those around you for help in squashing your fears.

When you have fears of abandonment, you can't place the responsibility on others to make you feel secure. Recognize your controlling behaviors that are a result of your fears, and prevent yourself from latching on to the unhealthy behaviors that you're so used to doing.

Remind yourself of the cause of those fears and how they are no longer needed for your emotional health. To the contrary, holding onto those fears only hinders you.

I must repeat to you that self-talk is incredibly powerful. It helps shape the way you think about yourself, as I mentioned earlier. Are you allowing your negative self talk to wallow in your fears, doubts, and insecurities about yourself? If so, it's time to replace those thoughts with some positive self-talk.

The goal with positive self-talk is not to focus on the relationship as that's not the cause of your fear of abandonment. Your fear of abandonment is built on feelings of unworthiness which transpired because of abandonment earlier in life. You need to replace your negative, fearful, anxious thoughts with positive self talk about yourself.

Remind yourself that you are worthy. Seek positive attributes in yourself that are worthy of admiration, and refocus on these when you feel emotions about fear of abandonment taking over. Banish the ugly feelings of fear by replacing them with positive thoughts about yourself: you're valuable, you're worthy and although you don't deserve the feelings of abandonment, you don't need to cling on to that fear.

Come to accept the idea that it's okay to be alone. You don't need another person in your life in order to be a valuable person. If you have a relationship that ends, then take that opportunity to embrace your being single. Find yourself. Do things to nourish you that you weren't able to do in a relationship. Don't fear being alone - your worth isn't based on your relationship status.

This leads on to my next (very important point): stop pursuing the emotionally unavailable. A lot of people with fear of abandonment issues can tend to seek out relationships with people who are emotionally unavailable. They often repeat this pursuit of emotional unavailability in each relationship they enter.

Instead of seeking the emotionally unavailable, break the cycle and seek out potential partners who are willing and emotionally able to hold a relationship with you. If you have a long pattern of chasing unhealthy, emotionally unavailable relationships, then recognizing this can be a breakthrough. Following through with this, and understanding you deserve someone available and ready for a relationship, can take some mindful work - but it's certainly achievable.

Those with fear of abandonment issues can become highly embedded in their relationships because of their habit to give too much and demand a great deal of their spouse or significant other's time. This causes other relationships to be neglected, and often turn sour.

Chapter Four - Why is My Mother a Narcissist?

A huge part of my healing process was to figure out why my mother was a narcissist. I didn't want to just assume she was inherently evil or her character was full of harmful flaws from birth - I realized that in order to fully heal, I needed a thorough understanding. I needed this question answered - *why is my mother a narcissist?*

Part of me wanted to find something to answer this question to help assure me that I wasn't the problem. Part of me needed to know that no matter what, nothing would have stopped my mother treating me the way she did. Another part of me also wanted to find a reason to feel sorry for her; for there to be something to almost excuse her for her vile treatment of me.

Of course, no matter the reason for her treatment of me, there isn't an excuse for it. Narcissists aren't psychopaths, therefore they do understand right from wrong.

However, our narcissistic mothers didn't develop their narcissism overnight. There isn't a one size fits all reason for why narcissistic mothers become the harmful parents they do, but I did find out a number of reasons that can help explain what would drive a mother to act so horrible towards her child.

The first reason could be **environmental factors**, particularly during her childhood. At first, I dismissed this as absolutely not being the case with my mother, as I always thought of her upbringing as idyllic. My nana was someone I adored, albeit a creature of habit and riddled with anxiety, she was someone I craved to be around when I was younger. At times I almost envied my mother for having my nana bring her up. I wanted to be brought up by my grandparents.

However, after looking a little deeper into this theory, I found that you don't necessarily need to have a narcissistic parent in order to become one. Factors such as family dynamics, parenting style, and childhood experiences can often have a significant effect on the child who later grows up to become a narcissistic mother. These things alone, or combined, can set the tone for future mental health, personality development and mental wellbeing (or often lack thereof).

When seeking the answers to what makes a mother narcissistic, and delving deeper into the theory that the environment helped create that narcissistic mold, I took a closer look at the harmful parenting styles that encourage narcissism.

The first style is '**authoritarian parenting**':

Parents who have an authoritarian parenting style are overly controlling, highly demanding, and are sluggish to give approval. Their style of parenting is deficient in warmth and affection, and they rarely show enough trust in their children to give them the space they require to grow and make their own mistakes in life.

Due to their style being more critical and domineering than empathic, authoritarian parents don't build their children's self-esteem, self-confidence, or nourish their ability to feel empathy for others. Their extreme demands produce highly insecure offspring, and as they grow older, they may go on to develop narcissistic personality traits, which serves as a coping mechanism.

The child of such parents will, in adulthood, go on to mirror the behavior of their parents, and may even recreate their personalities thinking that it's normal.

The next possible damaging style of parenting is '**indulgent parenting**':

This style of parenting is on the opposite end of the spectrum from authoritarian parenting. Overly indulgent parents have a tendency to praise and coddle their children incessantly. This is usually as a way to keep them pacified, but also often the indulgent parent truly believes their children deserve to put on a pedestal.

The indulgent parent doesn't set clear standards for their children to live up to. They create confusion by offering compliments and attention no matter of their behavior or performance.

Persistent praise and indulgent attitudes from parents can lead to inflated egos in their children, who then grow up into adults who believe they can do no wrong.

As well as this, if children sense that their parents won't discipline them or put boundaries in place because they don't care enough to do so, their self-esteem may be distorted and they may develop cynical and unsympathetic attitudes towards others. In cases like this, indulgence is a mask to cover up the emotional detachment the parent feels.

Indulgent parenting develops a child with an exaggerated sense of self, and strips them of the trust of others, ensuring they don't develop a healthy dose of empathy.

The final parenting type that can breed narcissism in their offspring is **pathological parenting**.

This type of parenting is what I assumed would automatically create a narcissistic child, and it's why I was certain that my nana's parenting style had no effect on the way my mother turned out.

In researching the above parenting style, I discovered that exposure to physical, emotional, and sexual abuse during childhood is a common theme for lots of people diagnosed with mental health issues, including those with a narcissistic personality disorder.

Again, the narcissistic personality traits are used as a coping mechanism by the adult who endured an abusive childhood.

Other environmental factors also help shape the adult the child will grow into. Alongside the parenting styles outlined above, bullying and rejection from peers can also cause a narcissistic personality to develop. The torment, verbal or physical assaults and antisocial behavior aimed at them can fester inside of them, and help contribute to them becoming a narcissistic adult.

I believe this was, for the most part, the case with my mother, alongside some 'authoritarian parenting' from my nana, who had mellowed in this respect when it came to taking care of me, so I didn't see this side of her.

My mother was bullied for her love of ballet, and would have her little vanity case with her outfit stored in it vandalized, thrown on the floor and ruined by the other children. She wore quite thick glasses, which was also another target for bullies. One of her eyes was lazy, and she wore conservative 'old person' outfits which added to her torment as a teen. Boys would ask her out only to humiliate her.

Upon discovering this, I was filled with a sense of anger at those people for treating my mother in such a way. I felt protective of her. I hated to think that she had been made to feel so unworthy, so pointless and so rejected that she turned into a narcissist. Then it dawned on me that *she made me feel that exact same way*. Suddenly, my compassion turned to anger towards her, and sadly part of me thought "good enough for her" when I thought back to her tormented childhood. After digesting all of those negative emotions, and checking myself to not let them fester, I was then allowed myself to sit and reason about my mother's narcissism.

I wouldn't excuse it. I can't excuse it. But in order to move forward, I wanted to find out what led her down the narcissistic path, and her traumatic experience with her peers from such an early age right up until her mid-teens offered me some reasoning for her behavior towards me.

Again, I won't excuse it. She's not a psychopath. They can't tell the difference between right and wrong. Narcissists can, they just choose to not care about that.

That horrible thing your mother said about your job? She knew just how hurtful it was, but she just didn't care, as long as it evoked the reaction she wanted. That time your mother told other family members something personal about you? Again, she knew how hurt you'd be when you found out, she just wasn't bothered. Unlike psychopaths, narcissists are aware of consequences, they just don't care all that much.

The reason I was so intent on finding out why narcissistic mothers turn out the way they do was to find some foundation that I could build my healing upon. If I didn't, I would forever be questioning what I'd done so wrong as a child, or what I should have done better when I was growing up to make her love me. Knowing that her narcissism was something that had developed way before I came along, and was something I could never have controlled, helped me progress in my healing.

Part of the blame also went to my nana, who was guilty of being authoritarian and academically pushy with my mother. I always wondered why my mother seemed quite cold to my nana, and for a long time, I thought it was because my mother was jealous of how much my nana doted on me. Often my mother would screw up her face and say "your nana never treated me like that" or "she's trying to make up for being such a bad mother to me". At the time, I just thought these phrases were another facet of my mother's narcissism: blaming others for her own feelings and not being able to conceal her undeniable envy.

Now that I can look back at this in a much more diplomatic, compassionate and understanding way as an adult, there were some obvious things my nana unwittingly did to help mold my mother into the emotionally unstable parent she became. Couple this with the profound rejection and trauma she received at the hands of her peers for over a decade, a narcissistic mother was created.

****

I hope this book has helped introduce you to the narcissistic mother.

Drawing from my own upbringing and my experience with a narcissistic mother, I hope to have shed some light onto the effects a narcissistic upbringing can have. If you've resonated with them, ideally I'll have given you some tools to use to combat them.

Thank you for reading this book, and if you have taken some knowledge, encouragement and a more rounded outlook on the narcissistic mother, then it's served its purpose. If you'd like to leave a review, it would be greatly appreciated. Let me know your own experiences with a narcissistic mother if you feel comfortable enough.

You can also find me and some of my posts at escapethenarcissist.com, so do head over there for more of my books and some more narcissism related articles.

Once again, thank you for reading and I wish you all the support in your healing journey.

****

Lightning Source UK Ltd.
Milton Keynes UK
UKHW010932250721
387701UK00001B/102

9 781393 892458